SPIRIT PACK

Fiona Manners

Grosvenor House
Publishing Limited

This book is published by
Grosvenor House Publishing Ltd
Link House
140 The Broadway, Tolworth, Surrey, KT6 7HT.
www.grosvenorhousepublishing.co.uk

This book is a work of fiction. Any resemblance to
people or events, past or present, is purely coincidental.

A CIP record for this book
is available from the British Library

ISBN 978-1-80381-299-1

Introduction and Dedication

Golden Retriever Tam arrived in my life when I was in my mid-twenties and she was five and half. I had never had a pet before whereas she had always been one so my learning curve was rather steep. By the time she died ten years later I'd also acquired two cats and a husband.

Three decades have passed since then, all of them immeasurably enriched by the company of the dogs you are about to meet. They all needed new homes and came from various backgrounds; some had known histories, others didn't, some had lived in domestic environments, others hadn't. What they had in common was that they all needed time, consistency and love to adjust to a new life with me.

This book is dedicated to the spirits of those seven dogs, to my current two living ones and to the other humans who shared their lives and loved them – Brian, Dave and Bob. It is also dedicated to the all the wonderful staff and volunteers who look after animals that need to be rehomed.

Spirit Pack

There are currently seven Dogs in the Spirit Pack. They have just two things in common, and the first of these is that their time in the Living World is over. The second, much stronger bond is the one that formed and will always unite the Pack: all the Dogs have lived some of their Living World lives with Her. For some, this was for several years; for others it was just a couple.

One unfortunate lad spent just a few weeks of his short Living World life with Her, so never got the chance to visit Castle Beach. The other Dogs were luckier and, whilst with Her, they'd sniffed and snuffled around the tidal river estuary, raced along the endless sandy beach, and explored the high grassy dunes that soar up to the sentinel castle. It is here, where river and sea converge, that the Spirit Pack came into existence. Although the Dogs still sometimes like to mingle amongst the Living World visitors, their presence on the beach now goes mostly undetected. Just occasionally, they are glimpsed by an old or poorly dog whose time in the Living World is almost over. To all other humans and dogs, the Spirit Pack is invisible – except to Her.

Tam, whose soft golden fur perfectly matches the golden sand, was the first Dog to live with Her and, when her Living World life was over, return to the beach as a Spirit Dog. Straightaway, she'd recognised the place where she'd helter-skeltered up and down steep tracks, chased oystercatchers in the shallow waves, and learnt to let crabs go about their business unmolested. Sometimes on these trips they had been joined by three sandcastle-building little girls, and then Tam would abandon her play to position herself on watchful guard duty. Her protective instincts did not go away just because she became a Spirit, and sometimes ill-mannered Living World dogs who are frightening children or trying to steal picnics are suddenly stopped by an inexplicable painful nip to a back leg!

Although Tam was mostly happy to be back on the beach as a Spirit, she did sometimes feel lonely without any of her Living World friends. One day, though, she'd heard Her voice gently say, "Bye bye, lovely Allie, off you go. You'll find Tam on the beach."

A few moments later, a large shuffling grey shape with pointy ears slowly came into view on the sand. Even though Allie was unable to use her back legs properly, Tam approached her warily. She was greeted warily in return. Allie's reticence was quickly replaced by joy when she realised that her body was regaining its former strength, just as Tam's had when she'd first arrived in the Spirit World. The two rather serious and self-contained Dogs quickly became relaxed with each other, spending their days paddling in the sea and running on the beach's quieter areas before returning to their sheltered dens to watch the visitors' activities.

Not long after Allie's arrival, she and Tam heard Her voice softly encouraging a third Dog that was leaving the Living World to return to the beach. Soon a black shape materialized on the beach, a bit smaller than Allie, but with even pointier ears and the same useless back legs. Allie immediately recognised her Living World friend Zukie who, finding that she could now stand properly on all four of her legs, was hurtling excitedly towards her and Tam. Zukie's arrival added a new dimension to the Pack; more extrovert than the other two, she often plays with the visitors.

Many a Living World human gawps in astonishment to see their thrown frisbee apparently change direction in mid-air never imagining that, unseen by them, Zukie has caught it hoping to entice Allie, also unseen, into continuing their favourite game

Over a long period of time, Tam, Allie and Zukie came to assume that their Pack was complete and so were surprised when they heard Her voice sending on a fourth. Sure enough, yet another pair of pointy ears – one upwards and one sideways this time – and damaged back legs appeared. This time, though, they belonged to a large male whose teddy-bear good looks and friendliness with humans disguise an undesirable tendency to bully other dogs. When Tip saw the three Dogs approaching he tensed and, realising his strength was returning, immediately hurled himself towards them, a blur of noise and menace. The impending assault would have taken Allie and Zukie completely off guard, but Tam recognised the threat.

Although smaller than Tip, she pulled her lips back into a tooth-filled, soundless snarl, and glared ferociously at him.

The defensive posture stopped Tip long enough for Allie and Zukie to surround and subdue him. From then on, he begrudgingly accepted the Pack's authority, although Tam still occasionally has to steer him away from intimidating nervous Living World dogs.

Another arrival came very quickly after this and was entirely unexpected. Snuffling in the dunes, Tam had heard Her voice, urging her, "Please find Stripe. He left so suddenly that I didn't get to say goodbye, and he's so weak. He's never been to the beach, but I'm sure he's there somewhere."

Suddenly alert, Tam noticed something on the sand ahead of her; a motionless dog-shaped shadow that feebly moved its narrow head when she softly nudged it. Unable to coax any further sign of life from it, she returned to the dens to get help. By the time Allie and Zukie got to him, it seemed as though Stripe might not even have enough strength to be a Spirit Dog. They snuggled around him, gently licked his wounds, and encouraged him to stay with them. Eventually he responded and tentatively stood, lanky legs shakily supporting a young and bony frame. Stripe's long body, black other than a white stripe on his chest, ended in a whip-like tail that he soon wagged so enthusiastically he almost knocked himself off his feet again.

It became evident that he had fully recovered his strength as he returned to the dens with Allie and Zukie. On seeing Tam and Tip waiting for them, and before any of them could react, Stripe took off.

He sprinted along the beach faster than they'd ever seen a dog run, long neck stretched forward as his paws thumped into the sand to propel him on at a fantastic speed.

The other Dogs watched amazed as, without slowing, Stripe raced in a huge, elongated circle, the same shape as the stadiums he'd been accustomed to. He returned to flop down in front of them in an exhausted, sweaty, and sandy heap.

The Pack knew about number six's arrival, but were surprised to find that Brindle – slight with a brown and black striped coat and fierce eyes – did not recover her Living World strength. As a young dog, Brindle's back legs had been badly injured, so she'd never walked properly. By the time she had gone to live with Her, she was quite old, and those legs were beyond recovery in both the Living and the Spirit Worlds.

Brindle's physical frailty is made up for by her feisty attitude and, with her fast reflexes and sharp teeth, she quickly saw off Tip's early attempts to intimidate her.

Brindle was pleased when the Pack heard that Apache, who had been her friend in the Living World, was to join them. He was, like Stripe, a former racing dog; less skinny, but still tall and pointed, his white coat splodged with dark patches.

Apache had been told by Her that Brindle would be waiting for him on Castle Beach, but she hadn't been strong enough to go with the others to meet him. When he saw five unfamiliar Dogs approaching, he'd been terrified and, like Stripe, had started to run. Unlike Stripe, Apache had been with Her long enough in the Living World to learn to run in a straight line, but unfortunately, his straight run took him straight off the flat beach and straight into the sea. By the time he finally stopped, he was up to the top of his legs in water and, frozen with cold and fear, wasn't about to move again. The fast and strong outgoing tide started to pull his legs from under him, threatening to sweep him away when Allie, the strongest swimmer in the Pack, ran into the water.

She swam around him, nudged his body so that he turned to face the beach, and then gently prodded him forward to the safety of the shore. He has never again ventured off the dry sand!

And so, seven quite different Dogs have found their own ways to exist together as a Pack. Tam and Tip alternately spar for dominance then, when Tam wins, play together chasing the still cormorants off their rocky perches. Allie dashes in and out of the sea, ineffectively attempting to catch the cuddy ducks in the shallow waves, whilst Zukie races around on the beach, happy to be close to her. Stripe and Apache relive old memories, sprinting together around a huge imaginary stadium. And Brindle? Well, Brindle simply lies comfortably in her cosy den, watching rather than being part of the activity and not begrudging or envying their energy.

When the Living World visitors have gone, the castle softens into shadow, the lighthouse on the nearby island sends its lifesaving beam out over the sea, and the beach settles into stillness. Then the Spirit Dogs return to their soft sand-grass dens, secure in the knowledge that they live on in Her heart and that, when Her time in the Living World is over, they will all be reunited on Castle Beach.

The Spirit Pack

Tam – Golden Retriever (born 1980), lived with Her 1985-1995

Allie – German Shepherd (born 1993), lived with Her 1995-2003

Zukie – German Shepherd (born 1993), lived with Her 1995-2003

Tip – German Shepherd (born 2001), lived with Her 2003-2010

Stripe – Greyhound (born c.2008), lived with Her 2010

Brindle – Greyhound (born c.2003), lived with Her 2012-2014

Apache – Greyhound (born c.2005), lived with Her 2010-2016

'Oh, my dead dears!' – The ghosts of his dead companions
appear to Blind Captain Cat – from *Under Milk Wood* by
Dylan Thomas

Still with Her in the Living World

Meg & Kye – Lurchers (born c.2012), living with Her 2016-

Lightning Source UK Ltd.
Milton Keynes UK
UKHW020632091222
413613UK00003B/41

9 781803 812991